Sinatra NOTHING BUT THE BEST

ISBN 978-1-4234-5949-1

HAL•LEONARD®
CORPORATION

7777 W. BLUEMOUND RD. P.O. BOX 13819 MILWAUKEE, WI 53213

Visit Hal Leonard Online at
www.halleonard.com

COME FLY WITH ME

Words by S...
Music by JAMES ...

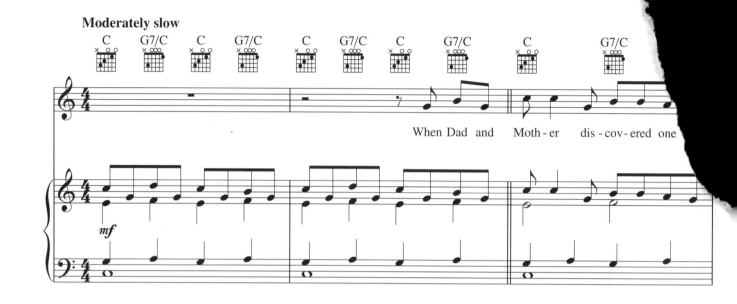

Moderately slow

When Dad and Moth - er dis - cov - ered one

oth - er, they dreamed of the day when they would love and hon - or and o -

bey. And dur - ing all their mod - est spoon - ing,

THE BEST IS YET TO COME

Music by CY COLEMAN
Lyrics by CAROLYN LEIGH

THE WAY YOU LOOK TONIGHT

from SWING TIME

Words by DOROTHY FIELDS
Music by JEROME KERN

LUCK BE A LADY
from GUYS AND DOLLS

By FRANK LOESSER

yet be-fore this eve-ning is o-ver, you might give me the brush. __ You

might for-get your man-ners, you might re-fuse to stay, and so the best that I can do is

Brightly, in 2

pray. _____

Luck be a la-dy to-night. _____

BEWITCHED
from PAL JOEY

Words by LORENZ HART
Music by RICHARD RODGERS

He's a fool and don't I know it, But a fool can have his charms;

I'm in love and don't I show it, Like a babe in arms.

Love's the same old sad sen - sa - tion, Late - ly I've not slept a wink,

THE GOOD LIFE

Words by JACK REARDON and JEAN BROUSSOLLE
Music by SACHA DISTEL

FLY ME TO THE MOON
(In Other Words)

Words and Music by
BART HOWARD

THE GIRL FROM IPANEMA
(Garôta de Ipanema)

Music by ANTONIO CARLOS JOBIM
English Words by NORMAN GIMBEL
Original Words by VINICIUS DE MORAES

Tall and tan and young ___ and {love - ly, the girl ___ } {hand - some, the boy ___ } from I - pa - ne -

- ma goes walk - ing, and when ___ {she pass - es, each one ___ she} {he pass - es, each girl ___ he} pass - es goes

"a-a-h!" ___ When {she walks she's} {he walks he's} like ___

SUMMER WIND

English Words by JOHNNY MERCER
Original German Lyrics by HANS BRADTKE
Music by HENRY MAYER

40

STRANGERS IN THE NIGHT
adapted from A MAN COULD GET KILLED

Words by CHARLES SINGLETON and EDDIE SNYDER
Music by BERT KAEMPFERT

Stran- gers in the night _____ ex- chang- ing glanc- es, won- d'ring in the night _____ ____ what were the chanc- es we'd be shar- ing love _____ be- fore the night was through. _____ Some- thing in your eyes _____ was so in- vit- ing,

MY KIND OF TOWN
(Chicago Is)

Words by SAMMY CAHN
Music by JAMES VAN HEUSEN

Don't ev-er, ev-er ask me what Chi-ca-go is, un-less you've got an hour or two or three. 'Cause I need time to tell you what Chi-ca-go is,

CALL ME IRRESPONSIBLE

from the Paramount Picture PAPA'S DELICATE CONDITION

Words by SAMMY CAHN
Music by JAMES VAN HEUSEN

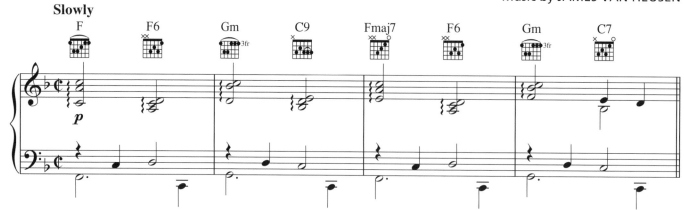

Call me ir-re-spon-si-ble, call me

un-re-li-a-ble, throw in un-de-pend-a-ble,

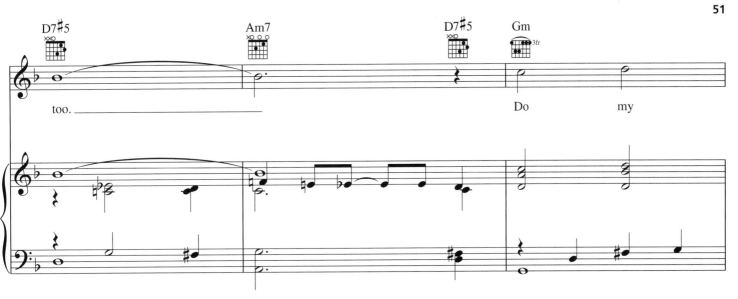

too. _____ Do my

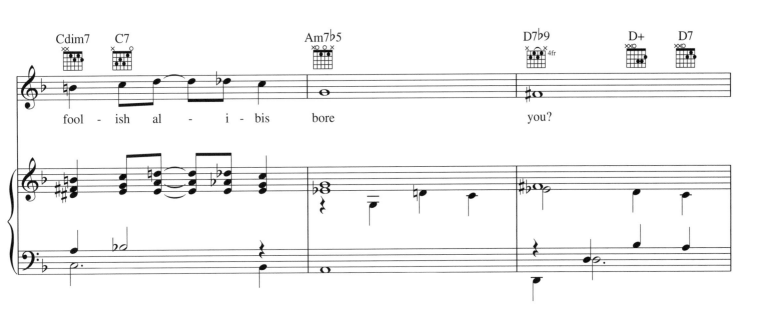

fool - ish al - i - bis bore you?

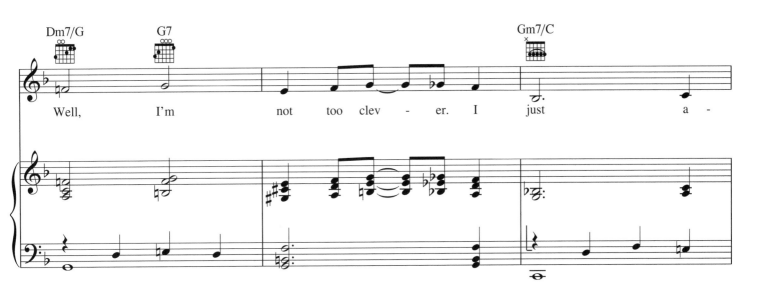

Well, I'm not too clev - er. I just a -

SOMETHIN' STUPID

Words and Music by
C. CARSON PARKS

Moderately slow

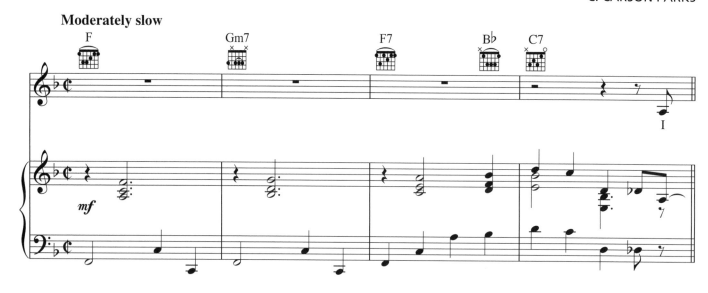

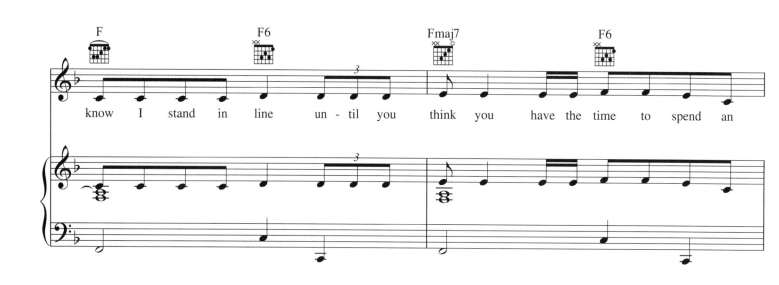

know I stand in line un - til you think you have the time to spend an

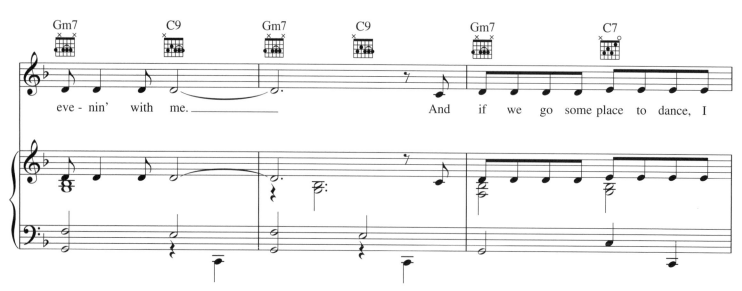

eve - nin' with me. _____ And if we go some place to dance, I

IT WAS A VERY GOOD YEAR

Words and Music by
ERVIN DRAKE

When I was   sev - en - teen, _____   it was a
twen - ty - one, _____   it was a
thir - ty - five, _____   it was a
days are   short, _____   I'm in the

ver - y good   year, _____   it was a ver - y good   year   for
ver - y good   year, _____   it was a ver - y good   year   for
ver - y good   year, _____   it was a ver - y good   year   for
au - tumn of the   year; _____   and now I   think   of my   life   as

THAT'S LIFE

Words and Music by DEAN KAY
and KELLY GORDON

MOONLIGHT SERENADE

Words by MITCHELL PARISH
Music by GLENN MILLER

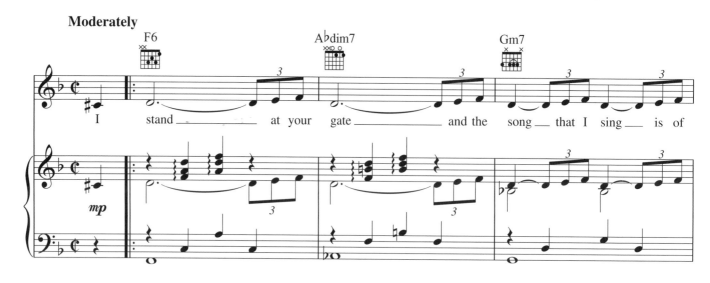

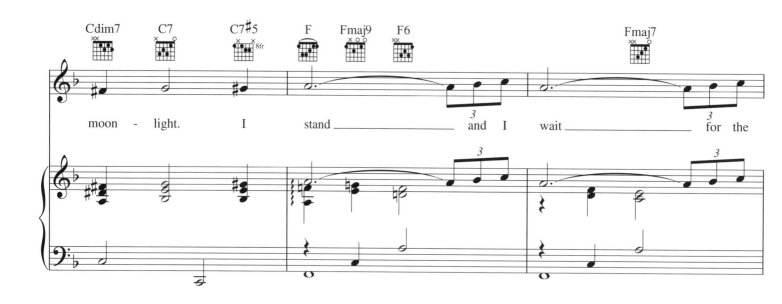

NOTHING BUT THE BEST

Words and Music by
JOHN ROTELLA

Recorded a half step lower.

DRINKING AGAIN

Words by JOHNNY MERCER
Music by DORIS TAUBER

ALL MY TOMORROWS

Words by SAMMY CAHN
Music by JAMES VAN HEUSEN

D.S. al Coda

there at my side, ___ I'll soon be turn-ing the tide, ___ just wait! As

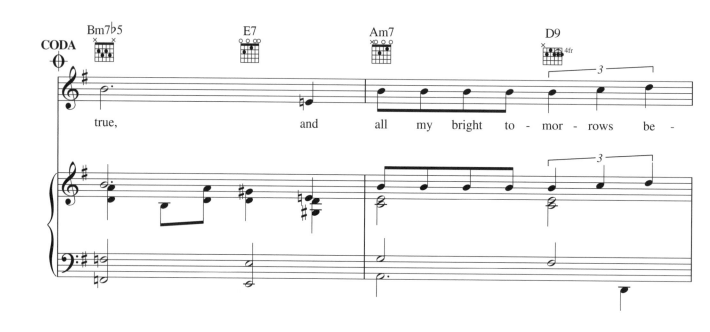

CODA

true, and all my bright to-mor-rows be-

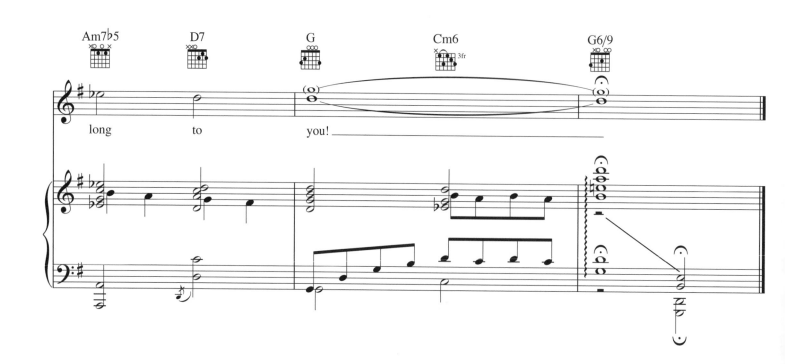

long to you! _____

THEME FROM "NEW YORK, NEW YORK"

Words by FRED EBB
Music by JOHN KANDER

BODY AND SOUL

Words by EDWARD HEYMAN,
ROBERT SOUR and FRANK EYTON
Music by JOHN GREEN

MY WAY

English Words by PAUL ANKA
Original French Words by GILLES THIBAULT
Music by JACQUES REVAUX and CLAUDE FRANCOIS